My Body is a Haunted House

Christina Marie Brown

My Body is a Haunted House

Christina Marie Brown

My Body is a Haunted House

ISBN: 978-1-7775401-0-4

My Body is a Haunted House

My Body is a Haunted House

This is dedicated to everyone who has stood by me while I have been learning to navigate the new truths about my body.

Thank you.

My Body is a Haunted House

Dear Reader,

In February of 2019 I was diagnosed with Endometriosis. I spent years never knowing the reason for a lot of my health issues. Between stomach problems, lower back pain, heavy painful periods, painful intercourse, brain fog, painful bowl movements, diarrhea and constipation, bloating, constant fatigue, and just a general feeling of nausea.

In the time since my diagnosis, I engulfed myself in writing poetry again. Learning to understand my feelings and thoughts about my new life. New diet, new medication, and new symptoms from the medication. Which Included massive weight loss (that was extremely unhealthy for me), depression, anxiety, and lowered libido.

Chronic illnesses can flip a person's life upside down. Even though a person lives with it every day, this does not mean that person's condition is not serious. I hope through this collection you may learn what life with a chronic illness can look like. Or at least learn what Endometriosis can look like.

My endometriosis is nowhere near as bad as some individuals. My struggle is my own and every person's experience is slightly different.

My Endometriosis is growing on my bowels. Knowing this can help provide context for some of my symptoms, and issues that plague my everyday life. For me, Birth control and an anti-inflammatory diet does wonders for symptom control. As a disease that is currently uncurable, symptom control is the best option right now.

I hope you enjoy this look into my life with Endometriosis and remember that every experience is unique. I hope we can move to a future where we validate women and their health concerns. A lot of women's health is under researched and from personal experience I can say that women are often not taken seriously regarding their health.

Love,

Christina Marie Brown

My Body is a Haunted House

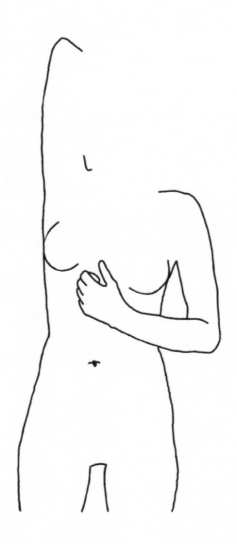

Diagnosis

A feeling from deep inside.

A flare gun shot into the sky.

Chronic Illness

Chronic illness.

The words feel foreign in my mouth.

Like I'm telling a lie.

How could I?

Someone so young,

have been stung?

The mirror doesn't reflect.

The mirror doesn't detect.

There is pain inside.

Like a constant, never ending, roller coaster ride.

A pretty shell

for something rotten.

                                        Chronic.

Humble Beginnings

Pop

Crack

Crunch

My hip makes these sounds sometimes when I find myself in motion.

These bones make audible reminders that this body doesn't function like a 20-something-year-old body.

Too young.

No one wants to hear how a 20-year-old is not sexy.

No one wants to hear about the long list of problems a body can have.

Too young.

I am too soon from the womb to have these pains. I am told I will learn my body with time.

I say, how I do know my body. We are together every passing moment. How do I not know my body? Every nook and crevice, a part of me. Every freckle, every scar, every mark is another star. Constellations mapped across my solar system.

Our bodies are our world within worlds. How do I not know the cosmos of my being?

Too young.

Broken I

Tight chest.

Maybe it's time to address,

the fog that has settled and floats around my head.

Loose thoughts lose thoughts.

Like water through my fingertips.

Like broken glass I cannot hold.

Like broken thoughts and broken dreams.

Like blood stains on bed sheets.

Looking through the smoke and haze,

looking through a clouded maze.

Trying to connect the dots,

connect all of these lost thoughts.

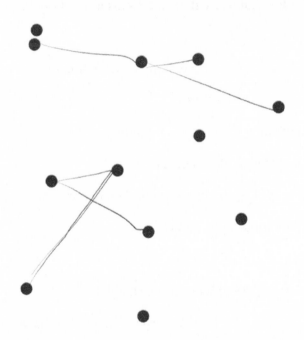

My Medication Gives Me Anxiety

My medicine causes anxiety.

Something I must now learn to live with.

I have always been a confident person;

but

now I feel it there

just beneath the surface.

Under the skin.

Lurking.

Itching.

Maybe if I scratch and pick, I will dig it out.

It never leaves:

the uncertainty.

Haunting

My body is a haunted house.

I am constantly haunted by the terrors of this body.

The jump scares of every day, waking up to a
different symptom wreaking havoc to this body.

What will go wrong today?

Your body may be a temple, but mine is a haunted
house.

Filled with ghouls and demons that somehow made
space for themselves.

My belly bloats and pushes as they swarm my
insides.

And the fog rolls in and clouds my mind.

I scream "I want them out".

But there is no exorcism in sight.

Broken II

Life slips,

loose grips,

holding my own hand.

Taking sips,

dim lights,

a losing fight.

Try to wake me up again.

Feeling faded,

times debated,

foggy head,

not much said.

        Time be greedy, taking sins.

I'm searching for the feeling;

the feeling of feet in the sand.

The hot and warm and comforting feeling;

but right now, I still have sandy feet.

Wet and muddy and cold.

My Medication Gives Me Anxiety II

My voice shakes.

Heart quickens,

breathing heavy,

palms are sweaty,

the room spins.

Bile.

In my mouth.

Swallow.

Smile.

Blink 3 times.

I can feel my pride fighting with the thing that now lives inside us.

For dominance.

Sometimes I win;

I'm in control,

I'm myself.

Sometimes?

I lose.

Shaking-

No,

vibrating.

I excuse myself.

Compulsive Behaviour

Itching

Scratching

Picking

Blood

Tear

Rip

Bleed

Scab

Pick

Scar

Itch

Scratch

Dig

Peel

Chew

Bite

Bleed

Again, again.

Skeleton

These bones ache and creak.

Whining at their existence beneath my skin.

Sometimes I think calcium supplements are not enough.

Oil me up like the Tin Man,

Help me move smoothly again.

This skeleton is fragile.

This skeleton feels like it is on fire.

Every crack sounds like it too.

But somehow there is no warmth here,

bone rubs on bone and yet there is no spark.

There is no flame, just the cracking of a fireplace.

Broken III

Restless is my mind

but it is even cloudier.

Side Effects Include: Lowered Libido

Some people feel the hunger.

They go into the night to hunt,

to subdue their needs.

Lust.

This word has lost all meaning.

In that, I find serenity and also, I feel lonely. The detachment to feeling these needs can be consuming.

Exhausting.

Loss lust.

Lust less.

I am.

I am.

What does it take to form human connection to the significant other?

What does it take to live not in pain, but also not in lust?

Does this new quiet suit me? Do I wear it well?

Secrets only whispered between the bedsheets with my lover, who can tell. My lover who can tell me all these hidden little truths, nuggets of good will.

Side effects include: lowered libido.

Loss lust.

Lust less.

I am.

I am.

My Medication Gives Me Depression

My medication causes depression.

It's like walking through deep water-

          -No

Under water.

The fish seem happy, but I cannot breathe.

Chronic Pain or Anxiety?

The anxiety is really consuming.

And I'm not talking what people *call* anxiety,

when what they mean is *stress.*

I'm talking about picking at your skin until you
bleed but needing the repetitive action.

I'm talking not being afraid, but your body won't
stop shaking so violently you make yourself sick.

I'm talking being physically sick and throwing up
over something you've done 100 times.

I'm talking forgetting how to breathe or
hyperventilating over something so small, it was
never a problem.

I don't mean stress.

I mean my medication causes anxiety

and I know the difference.

The doctors said it causes anxiety

and depression.

I know stress. I have always been the loud and annoying.

And now I hide in my car to avoid interaction.

The paranoia gets to me so bad I lock all the doors.
Of the house, of the car, everywhere. Afraid and
vividly aware. I count, and I tap, and I fidget just to
hold back

the vomit

that permanently sits in my throat.

I remind myself

who I am

and how this is not it.

I remind myself the difference of stress.

Of feeling stressed and overwhelmed to make a
phone call

verses the panic I feel in calling someone I want to
talk to.

The absolute fear of just getting a text message.

The slight vibrations of my phone and I am afraid.

They made me pick between chronic pain or anxiety.

Bloom

This body is a desolate place.

Where there should be people waiting to be

there is nothing but rot.

Deep inside my being where there should be
flowers waiting to blossom and bloom,

they are wasted.

Eggs that never hatch,

like seedlings that die after a late frost.

This body is empty, and I am alone.

Never will something or someone else share this
body as a home,

not even briefly.

How does one love a body that doesn't love them
back?

How does one welcome with open arms, self-love,
when the body attacks -

- itself?

Ghost I

There's a ghost in the house.

But,

I've learned that the house is me.

And the ghost is also me.

Dry Mouth

Dry mouth.

Blank thoughts.

Quick heart.

Breathing fast.

Why am I always standing here in this position?

My body is afraid, but my mind thinks of nothing.

Unmoving.

Unaware.

Unmotivated.

Where is the source of this anxiety induced physical reaction?

Where is my logic and critical thought getting me now?

Here.

                                        There.

Nowhere.

Bloat

34 degrees in the middle of July.

In nothing but my underwear so I stare at my thighs.

The lines on the skin akin to the lines on my arms;

white lines, white lies.

I am bloated and fat.

I am hurting.

Everything I do makes my stomach swell.

Makes my stomach expand.

Trying to leave my body, be set free;

to be free of me.

I try to do that too sometimes.

I want to leave this body and separate me, from me.

My stomach will growl and yell in protest and it
never gets away from me, trapping the beast inside.

I use to make jokes something evil lived in my stomach and caused all this pain, but I was wrong, the demon lives in my ovaries, my uterus, and it is consuming my bowels, and the demon never sleeps. The demon is real and lives inside me.

I just want to separate me, from the demon.

Rot made a home inside my body

Disassociation / lost my association / with myself /
my body / body blurring / glitch in the system

Maze

What is a body?

I feel it all too soon, the crushing loneliness of
owning a body,

A maze of bone and tissue I still cannot navigate.

Caught in the trap.

I have always felt out of place in this flesh.

And I am reminded I don't know how to pray,

I try religion on like a sexy cocktail dress

never finding my size.

I sip on religion like top shelf liquor, but it still
burns my throat.

None of them are the key that fits,

None of them realign my body with my soul.

And each passing year my body has new
discoveries,

They say you can't discover land that's already
inhabited-

      - so, my body makes new land, pulling
ghosts out of time and weaving them to my insides.

And I find my myself washed ashore, unexplored-

        -worlds now at my fingertips

What a glorious maze it has built.

Attaching my intestines together and together to
my-

                                    home?

(can a uterus be a home?)

How can I compete

with a body against me?

This is where I knew I was falling.

Caught in a trap.

What seems like new horizons as my body expands,
all it expands is the bloat in my stomach, and the
pain in my back, and the fears in my heart.

As it tears me apart,

or tears itself apart.

It is so hard not to lose yourself in your disease.

I am not this body and I have never felt at home
here.

This body is mine, but we are not one.

It makes choices I didn't consent to, as we share the
same void. Taking up the same space on physical
planes,

I did not consent to.

(a uterus is a home)

But my home is rotten.

Chronic Illness in Regard to Women's Health

They say I'm beautiful because I'm sick,

but they won't help me through the chronic.

"Women with your illness

are much more attractive."

But how does that help me

get rid of all the extra pieces?

I don't care about these studies.

Give me something with progress.

I grow tired of the objectification of women,

sitting in doctor offices, waiting to be given a
diagnosis.

Too pretty to be sick, or too fat to be anything else?

Or maybe I am too skinny today and that will be the
chosen blame.

When did my sex determine how you approach me in medicine?

I find these studies disgusting.

Finding me attractive will not remove the disease plaguing the insides of my body. Finding me attractive will not release me from never ending pain. Finding me attractive will not cure the uncurable. Finding me attractive does not make me fertile. Finding me attractive does not help the chronic.

Here is my diagnosis:

- A system riddled with sexism.
- A system not focused on progress.

progress, progress, progress

Bloat II

The bloat in my abdomen swells and pushes the skin.

It's painful to move.

Painful to breathe.

Flesh & Bone

I want you to separate me from it.

Take away the flesh and bone.

I am not it.

My body hides a dark truth.

Invisible to the eyes.

My body knits and weaves with my insides.

I feel homesick for the body I knew before.

Before I knew about all this extra tissue.

Something About Weight

I grew so tired of sitting on the toilet.

Now I am tired of explaining my diet.

No matter the sin, I remain so frail and thin

The demons on my insides scream in pain with each bite of forbidden fruit I want to consume.

"Cut them out." They say.

The demons' slumber when temptation is withheld. But my stomach becomes a bottomless pit. That a diet without carbs, cannot be filled. I eat and I eat and I shed away pounds. How can I eat so much and still lose more weight?

The skin clings to my bones, and I feel myself shrinking.

How can that be when my body is expanding?

The demons shed and somehow produce, more of me for all of you to love.

But you don't love.

A bloated tummy with tiny thighs.

skinny, skinny, skinny

My body is my demise.

My Body is a Haunted House

Isolation

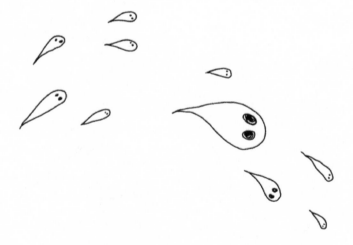

Christina Marie Brown

Bath Fix

The bath fixes everything

From my achy hips

To the words from his lips

Just Listen.

Listening is a sign of respect.

Show me some and don't make me repeat myself.

Who am I Now?

I was so happy when I realized who I was.

I spoke and acted unapologetically and authentically as myself.

I did not fear repercussions.

As long as I was true to myself

and who I am.

I sparked courage and inspiration in many I touched,

but

then I fell away

and lost who I was again.

It is like being reborn, when you learn something new about yourself.

When I learned I, myself, turned on me.

My body was against me.

That my choice to not be a mom, was never actually
a choice.

My freedoms to choose were ripped away from me.

And suddenly I wanted a child I would never have.

And suddenly I found myself shaking at 2 a.m.
always over the same thing.

Why?

Why would my own body turn against me?

Something that made me feel empowered

now made me feel wrong.

Something I pictured blossoming inside

was actually trying to die.

I just want to know who I am now.

Who I have always unknowingly been.

I learn the feelings I had, and the weight of life was
all symptoms of something rotten inside.

I learn that I can feel better while somehow also feeling worse.

I learn that I am not who I thought I am

And now I don't think I will ever have the confidence to know who I am ever again.

Just Listen Please

I try to explain my struggles with mental health to those who do not know me as someone with these struggles.

I try to explain it is a symptom from medication, medication that has benefits that outweigh my mental health.

Medication that is working. Mental health I track for my doctor, my specialist.

I try to explain.

But people don't fully hear.

I have had, people respond, projecting their own issues onto me.

Telling me what mental illness I have.

Telling me why I have it.

Telling me how to fix it.

That they will fix it.

Fix me.

But they don't listen.

They are so busy wanting to be listened to themselves, they forget to listen to others.

ways I combat my depression

After Maddie McGlinchey

I wrap myself in blankets / these warm fuzzy layers
protect me from the world / I burn incense / and
make tea / even if I don't drink it / I remind myself
to drink water / I put on my favourite pajamas / the
ones that make me happiest / I throw everything out
/ the purging of material is a substitute for purging
myself / I remind myself it is just the medicine / I
count all the reasons my medication matters most / I
read poetry / the sadness is so consuming I seem to
only be able to read it and not write it / I stare at
screens / screens stare back at me / laugh tracks play
in the background / I call my mom / or she calls me
/ I'm not sure anymore / I make hamburger helper
from scratch / and I bake everything I have ever
saved in my recipe book / I paint flowers into
greeting cards and write someone a note to remind
myself how much I love them / how much they love
me / I take selfies / empty voids stare back at me
from the photos / why do I only take photos when I
am tired? / I cry / and I cry and I cry and I cry / until
I just sleep and I sleep and I sleep / rinse and repeat

Opera - Thinking about how much I love my mom

My mother has always known me

but sometimes I wish she knew me.

Sometimes there feels like there's this gap

and I can't just reach out.

Sometimes there feels like there's these voids
between people

that I can't seem to fill.

I sometimes feel lost looking in these voids.

Like a fog

but sometimes it's like drowning.

Sometimes I think of calling out

but the space just feels too far

and I lose sight of the shore.

So, I float on my back in the water

not sure if I'm happy anymore.

Ghost II

This body is not a home.

In it, I feel alone.

A ghost inside my own shell.

What am I?

If I don't belong

                here.

I feel like a captor to my own soul.

Caged within my own bone.

Locked away behind flesh and blood.

So, I cut it away and it does no good.

How long do I have to stare in the mirror to feel like I'm not trapped inside someone else?

How long do I have to stare in the mirror just feel something?

How long do I have to stare in the mirror before killing myself?

Silence

A deafening silence has settled around my mind. No words form or take shape in this darkening place. I wallow in the shallows of my depression. And ask myself what it is I'm suppressing. Out in the depths of this sea, I am only ankle deep but something out there is lurking.

I've always said depression feels like drowning.

Gasping for air. There is a peace and calm consuming.

And what if I float out into the deep water on my back. Then let myself sink once I get far enough out. What will I find at the bottom?

Mirrors

I am so bad at knowing people.

I think I see them for what they are.

But it's like a house of mirrors.

Always reflecting / never who they should be /
never where I think they are / how do I know this is
real / this feeling / this face / how do I find my way
out into the light / how do I find the right / person /
path / connection

I feel lost.

The map I made was wrong.

Untitled I

It hurts.

Being chronically ill.

It opens your life, for others to hate you for having an invisible illness.

I'll never forget the feeling of betrayal and the feeling of emptiness as he looked at me and said he was frustrated I was depressed.

A depression I could not lock away.

A depression nothing really made.

A depression from my medication.

How do you rebuild trust when they hate you because you're chronically ill?

Broken trust

Broken love

Broken body no one loves

Untitled II

How do you

just

step forward through that pain?

The pain of a lover who thought he could handle being there for you, through all of the struggles of the chronically ill.

To just brush past their resentments and let them feel heard.

When all you can hear is the betrayal in their voice.

A voice that use to drip with tenderness and love

but they haven't shown you that in months.

Months go by and they won't even touch you. Won't even caress you.

How do you brush it aside?

When you just want to be honest.

I believe honesty is the most important moral

but it doesn't mean I have to be okay with what you say.

```
Teaching me not to trust
again
```

You pull away.

I think you are doing what you always do.

But now I feel like we have played this on loop as a never ending rerun.

I think how long it has been since you last wanted to fuck me.

I think how every time I need you; you avoid me.

I think how I tried to talk about the symptoms of my medication, and I felt someone should help me, and I needed someone to be with me.

I think of how you lied to me and told me I didn't have depression; how many times you told me I was fine.

You lied.

You harbored all these feelings

and learned to hate me.

You hated me for the thing you said I didn't have. You discouraged me from getting help for the thing that made you despise me.

You told me I was fine because you yourself needed reminding.

I am not my disease and that's not how you should define me.

Don't Get Confused

Don't confuse my hugging you as forgiveness.

Don't confuse my tenderness as love.

Don't confuse my honesty as trust.

Don't confuse my openness with caring.

Don't confuse my hurt with disgust.

Don't confuse my disease as all of me.

The Other Me

I look through mirrors and try to see truth

buried beneath.

I always feel like there is another me.

Another layer.

talking ghosts / whispers in my ears

"you cannot carry us both"

They say as I try to unmask what is beneath.

Will I ever find serenity in knowing?

Sex in the Cemetery

Hold me down.

Look into my eyes.

Pour your soul over mine.

Just don't look to closely at my insides,

you'll see love and caring and rot.

Flip me over,

lay onto me.

Let me feel your teeth in my back.

Let me focus on that pain instead.

What does it feel like to fuck a graveyard?

All of these eggs, but I'm probably infertile.

```
You're being shaken up in
your bottle right now.
```

How am I trapped in the bottle and drowning in the sea?

I thought a bottle would float but maybe mine has no cork.

Tipped sideways, filling with water.

Washed out to sea and drown me.

I often find myself stuck in these places

Always caught in life's dramas

When will the water be finished having her way with me?

My bottle is shaken. I am a girl who often feels badly broken.

Dump the bottle upside down and pour me out.

Christina Marie Brown

My Body is a Haunted House

Christina Marie Brown

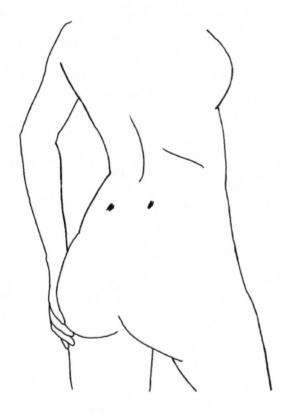

Acceptance

I don't want to be pure

I don't want to be sweet

I don't want to be nice

I don't want to be neat

Dandelions

I think I am a dandelion.

Sometimes I want to be a daffodil, or a tulip.
Something still resilient but daintier.

But I am the dandelion.

As beautiful as I may be, as much as I look like a
child of the sun.

I am despised and disgusted by many.

But I am strong and resilient. I will continue to
grow no matter the situation.

No matter how hard it may be.

My life may be the concrete, but I am growing in its
cracks.

I may be disposable, but I am still there for you
when you need me.

Dandelions have so much to offer and are so strong
in the face of adversity.

I sometimes wish to be more beautiful and more
desired, but I am already so beautifully perfect. And
I will survive.

Garnet Sea

The sheets are stained with everything the body has
ejected. Deep garnet marks the passage

- of time, of breath, of life

Of my life and how it has been so strongly affected,
by the overflow of symptoms trying to
communicate the magnitude of pain inside. But it
goes unlistened to as the gate opens wide and the
red sea emerges. Nothing slows the flow of the sea
or prevents it from seeping through or into
anywhere it can escape onto.

You catch me red handed as I scrub the stains from
so many different fabrics. Washed in blood
becomes a typical Tuesday evening.

And somehow now when red wine spills I am
reminded of these times. Garnet washed away as it
circles the drain. Only a few drops remain. Like
pomegranate seeds littering my sleeves. I stare
unsure what they mean. What are they telling me?

Ghost III

My body is filled with ghosts.

My body is a haunted house.

Somewhere deep in my abdomen

There is all the extra tissue

Tissue black and bad

signs of something gone   r o t t e n

I feel like these are ghosts. Not alive and not dead.

Just my body's attempt to shed

                                                itself.

They haunt me,

Every day and every night the haunting continues.

Instead of creaky floors, I have creaky bones.

Instead of foggy nights, I have brain fog.

And so, the ghosts continue.

But possession is quite alive in this body. My
endometriosis possesses me all the time.

The only exorcism for me lays under an excision.

A Letter to my Body

My horoscope tells me: "if there is something about yourself you don't like, then change it"

But how do I tell my horoscope that I cannot change my body?

I do not wake up each morning and carefully select one from a rack.

Bodies are not like pressed shirts, hanging, waiting to be picked.

Bodies are formed and melded (with consciousness)

and cannot be separate.

How do I change?

How do I change?

How do I change?

Untitled III

I had a nightmare

about having a baby

and I was almost thankful

since I know I probably won't carry.

What a burden it is, to carry all of these emotions? The weight of infertility digging its boney elbow into my back, and the heavy anchor of not really wanting to birth in the first place dragging my hands to the ground as I cling to it with every fingertip.

"Carry both burdens" I tell myself repeatedly, as if this somehow will bring justice onto my face, and onto my soul.

I carry both; and my arms grow stronger and my back straightens, and the fear of daylight breaks into night. I welcome the darkness, welcoming the nightmares to the mind.

Accepting what may or may never be. Washing myself in that tranquility of not knowing. Wash myself in peace with who I have happened to be. Wash myself in the relief; the relief of not having added another loss to the list of grievances. Yet I still grieve. I make space for grieving; like dancing in the moonlight by the lake – grieving can make you feel free.

Undead

WARNING UNDEAD AHEAD

I often think about all the pieces of me that could've brought life.

And how they are all waiting to just be shed.

Like undead.

Never to be alive but once filled with potential.

Filled with the capacity to bring life.

But I feel like these ovaries are graveyards. Housing things that will never be anything more or anything less.

Things that will just be blood exiting the body.

shedding, shedding, shedding

My life source never overflowing, breathing life into another being.

Empty and alone. Housing the very things that will be my downfall.

Brush away and remind myself, I am more than
what pieces of me could have been.

breathing, breathing, breathing

Exhale regret. Exhale fear.

Jupiter is the Largest Planet

The skin around my stomach stretches outward.
Pushing against itself

- me.

Call me Jupiter.

I am full of gas, and the bloat makes my body
unrecognizable.

Who are you?

Who am I today?

This version of myself is the largest of all the
versions of myself. I look at the solar system of all
the versions of me I have captured and framed;
hung on the walls of my brain;

She is the largest. The most distained.

Because of the pain

- the bloat

The things that come afterwards.

A foggy mind, and

- this body is a trap.

I am a balloon animal at a birthday party

and they don't know when to stop pumping air into me.

When will I burst?

Will I burst like the zit no one wants, or will I burst like a pinata? Will I explode to a crowd of cheers, for all the things hidden inside?

I am terrified, but also eagerly waiting to know the results.

Toothache

This was always written in the stars.

Woman ate the forbidden fruit,

and the toothache it caused, that took root.

The roots of that pain carry themselves generations.

Manifesting.

Manifesting like grievances we never knew we
would burden ourselves with.

Virgo, virgin mother, justice disguised.

My burden is my truth.

My burden is my womb.

But a woman is not the sum of her parts, and that
becomes a mantra. Said in the mirror at the start of
each day. The start of each rising dawn. The start of
each new beginning, being washed in blood. The
cycle, continuing.

Not the sum of parts.

Like a toothache it can be pulled out by its roots and removed. And someday when the cavity is too large that is what will be awaiting.

Dig up the whole plant. Mother Earth grew this in my body. All bodies rise from dirt and return to Earth. Dig out the whole plant. The planter of my abdomen will become too small to hold the black petal flower inside. My abdomen would then be picked clean and let the space be consumed by my other organs.

The night sky is still beautiful as I stare at a map of my own demise. Black holes and twinkling lights, matching the colour of my insides and the hope that has often found itself wandering in my eyes.

I make peace with these truths. I make peace with things I don't know.

A Bridge Between Heaven and Earth

I am learning to show my body tenderness.

I remind myself this body is a home, made from Earth and will return to dirt.

I am a being blessed with a home so warm that I carry myself within.

I remind myself of the magic this body can do. Weaving and creating. Spinning black gold flesh from nothing.

A bridge between Heaven and Earth.

Honest Hands Holding

My lover holds me in his honest hands

Holding me hostage in our home

Holy embrace, holding my soul in place.

Heaven or Hell hold me here.

Hold me even if the tide rises high.

Even if the night sky hitches a ride and day light
hums harmoniously into the hours of the morning.

Our humanity resting humbly in our heads.

A Letter to my Lover

Being with you makes my body sing.

I feel joy in every corner and crevice of my being -

vibrating

dancing

- and the laughter we share, continually rings in my ears.

You make sunrises worth getting up to (at all).

You make tasks that feel like burdens feel like sharing a secret;

a secret moment shared between us.

I sleep better with you beside me,

at least that's what I tell myself.

I know it is not true, I always am more rested alone;

But I'd rather not sleep well than face the loneliness of being without you, lover.

I want your hands tangled in my hair at 1:00 a.m. as we talk about trivial topics like the passing of each day.

I want to listen to your footstep retreat to the kitchen and fetch a glass of water.

I want to smell your bad breath warming the side of my face as it eventually wakes me up in the morning.

I want to squeeze into a bathtub much too small for the both of us, just to have an excuse to be together, ever closer.

I love you. I love you. I love you.

Sincerely,

My heart

Equanimity

Learning to live in this body feels like equanimity.

Like I am learning to make a home out of a sunset.

Like the taste of vanilla mixed with subtle regret.

Like listening to a record player unnoticeably skip.

Like erasing instincts as smoothly as I can

                              - delete, delete, delete

Like wearing borrowed expressions to hide the obsession with: Why is this body not what it's meant?

But loneliness is the fracture that never heals quite right.

And I will always be alone in this body.

My star sign was always the maiden,

The virgin.

I never thought in this meaning, it meant never bearing children.

There is no justice here.

There is no innocence here.

There is no purity here.

There is no precision here.

Just the subtle act of equanimity.

My Body is a Haunted House

My Body is a Haunted House

Acknowledgements

I want to thank my mom and dad for always pushing me to write. For always pushing me to pursue the arts, and my passions.

I need to thank my friends, who have always encouraged any endeavour I have dreamed of.

For the online community, the ones I have formed friendships with and for my followers. You all have reminded me I can, and I will.

For my lover, who stands by me even when things are trying. This is hard on me as it is you. Thank you for always pushing me to do the things I dream about.

For Alicja, Sabina, Hazel, and Maddie for being my advanced readers and showing me so much excitement and support. You're support and friendship through this process means more than words can say.

Thank you.

My Body is a Haunted House

About the Author

Christina Marie Brown is a writer currently living in Peterborough, Ontario. She fell in love with writing at a young age. Later finding poetry at age 10. Her poetry and prose focus around love, losing love, depression, and her experiences with the chronic illness Endometriosis.

Instagram: @mariebrown.poetry

My Body is a Haunted House

Christina Marie Brown

Made in the USA
Monee, IL
11 August 2021